MW00958230

God's Miracle Man

Told by Carine Mackenzie
Illustrations by Fred Apps

Published by Christian Focus Publications
Geanies House, Fearn, Tain, Ross-shire, IV20 1TW, Scotland
© 1994 Christian Focus Publications
Printed in Singapore

Elijah was a good man who loved the Lord God. God used him to speak to the people of Israel.

One day God told Elijah to warn King Ahab, 'There will be no rain or dew on the land for some years.' Ahab was angry with this bad news.

'Go east across the river Jordan and hide beside the brook Cherith,' God told Elijah.

Elijah drank water from the brook. Every morning
and every evening ravens brought bread and meat for
him to eat. God took care of Elijah in this lonely place.
   God takes care of us too. He gives us many good
gifts - food, clothing, shelter and friends.

When the brook dried up, God told Elijah to move on to Zarephath.

'There is a widow there who will feed you,' God said to him. When Elijah met the woman at the city gate, she was gathering sticks.

'Bring me a drink of water and a piece of bread,' he called to her.

'I have hardly any food left,' she told him. 'I am about to cook one last meal for myself and my son before we die of starvation.'

'Don't be afraid,' said Elijah. 'Go and cook the meal, but make a little cake for me first. God has told me that your barrel of meal and your jug of oil will not run empty as long as this drought lasts.'

The widow did as Elijah asked. She was amazed that the food and the oil lasted for as long as it was needed.

Some time later the widow's son died and she came to Elijah in great distress. Elijah carried the boy up to a bed in the room he used in the loft. He stretched himself out on top of the boy's body three times, and begged the Lord to restore him.

God heard Elijah's prayers. Elijah took the young boy back downstairs to his mother. 'Look,' he said, 'your son is alive.' The woman was overjoyed. 'Now I know that you are a man of God. The words of God that you speak are really true.'

The woman had done what she could by helping Elijah when he was hungry. God had repaid her far above her expectations.

We too should serve God by helping others in whatever way we can. God has promised that this service will be rewarded.

Obadiah, one of the chief servants of the king, loved and served God, like Elijah.

During the drought, King Ahab and Obadiah went out in different directions to search for grass for the horses and mules. On the way Obadiah met Elijah, who spoke to him. 'Go and tell the king that I am here,' said Elijah.

'Why?' replied Obadiah. 'The king has been looking for you for a long time. As soon as I tell him, the Spirit of God will carry you away to a secret place. When Ahab cannot find you he will be so angry that he will kill me instead.'

'I promise that I will not disappear. I will meet King Ahab.'

So Obadiah brought the king to meet Elijah. 'There you are, you troublemaker!' shouted Ahab.

'I am not a troublemaker,' replied Elijah. 'You and your father have caused trouble by not obeying God's commands. You have been worshipping the false god called Baal.'

Elijah offered a challenge. 'Let's have a contest between me and the prophets of Baal.'

So Ahab summoned all the Israelites and 450 prophets of Baal to meet at Mount Carmel.

Elijah addressed the crowd. 'If the Lord is the true God, you should worship Him; but if Baal is really God, you should worship him.' Nobody said a word.

Elijah then explained what was to take place. The God who accepted the sacrifice of a bull by fire would be the true, powerful God. The people roared their approval.

The prophets of Baal had their turn first. They took a bull and prepared it as a sacrifice on the altar. Then they danced round the altar praying to Baal.

Nothing happened.

At noon Elijah made fun of them. 'Perhaps Baal is busy. Perhaps he is sleeping. Shout louder to wake him up.'

The prophets of Baal shouted louder and louder till the middle of the afternoon. Still nothing happened. Baal had failed.

When it was Elijah's turn, the crowd of onlookers gathered closer. First he repaired the altar of the Lord with twelve big stones. Then he dug a trench around it. He put wood on the altar and then laid the prepared bull on top of it.

'Fill four jars with water and pour them over the offering and the wood,' he ordered.

The order was repeated four more times until wood and offering were soaking wet and the trench was filled with water.

Elijah prayed to God. 'O Lord, prove that you are the true God, and that I am your servant. Answer me, so that the people will know that you are God.'

The Lord sent down fire on the altar. It burnt up the sacrifice, the wood, the stones and the soil, and dried up the water in the trench. When the people saw this, they threw themselves on the ground and shouted, 'The Lord is God; the Lord is God.'

The prophets of Baal were destroyed.

The Lord had proved without doubt that he was the true God.

The Lord God is the only true God still. Jesus is the only way to God the Father. If we trust Him, He will be our friend. We can speak to Him any time.

Elijah told King Ahab, 'Go and have something to eat. I think it will rain soon, and the drought will be ended.'

Ahab went to eat, but Elijah climbed to the top of Mount Carmel to wait for the rain. 'Go and look out towards the sea,' he told his servant. 'I cannot see anything unusual,' was the reply.

Seven times Elijah repeated the order. The answer was the same until the seventh time. 'There is a little cloud coming out from the sea; it looks no bigger than a man's hand.'

'Go to King Ahab,' ordered Elijah, 'and tell him to set off for home before the rain stops him.'

Soon the sky was covered with dark clouds; the wind blew and heavy rain began to fall.

Ahab rode in his chariot back to the palace in Jezreel. The Lord gave Elijah special strength and he ran all the way to Jezreel in front of Ahab's chariot.

Jezebel, Ahab's queen was furious when she heard what had happened to the prophets of Baal. She threatened to kill Elijah. He was afraid and fled for his life to Beersheba in Judah.

All alone, Elijah walked into the desert. He sat down, tired and depressed under a tree.

'I may as well be dead,' he moaned, then he fell asleep. An angel touched him, saying 'Wake up and eat.' He ate, then fell asleep again. Again the angel woke him. 'Get up and eat, or you will not be strong enough for the journey.'

Elijah rose, ate and drank, then walked for forty days to Mount Sinai.

God was not angry with Elijah. He still cared for him when he was afraid and felt so alone. God has promised never to leave us. He is still watching over us when we feel alone.

Elijah was spending a night in a cave, when the Lord spoke to him, 'What are you doing here?'

'I am the only one left who serves you Lord. The people are trying to kill me,' Elijah replied sadly.

'Go and stand on the top of the mountain,' the Lord told him. A fierce wind blew and shattered the rocks. Then there was an earthquake, then a fire. But the Lord did not use these powerful forces to speak to Elijah. He spoke in a soft, whispering voice. When Elijah heard it, he had to cover his face with his cloak.

'What are you doing here Elijah?' the voice of the Lord said. Again Elijah replied, 'I am the only one left who serves you - people are trying to kill me.' But he was wrong.

'There are still 7,000 people alive in Israel who serve me,' said God.

Now Elijah had no need to be so sad.

God also told Elijah to appoint a man called Elisha to be prophet after him. When Elijah met Elisha he gave him his cloak as a sign that he was to be his successor.

King Ahab had plenty of possessions and land, but he had a great desire to own the lovely vineyard belonging to Naboth. Naboth did not wish to sell his family property. Ahab sulked.

Queen Jezebel hatched a wicked plot. She had Naboth killed and Ahab took the vineyard for himself.

Elijah faced up to Ahab in the vineyard. He warned him about the result of this evil behaviour. Sin always leads to trouble, but God tells us that if we confess our sin to him and are sorry about it, He will forgive us and cleanse us from sin.

After Ahab died, his son Ahaziah became king. He was just as wicked as his father and mother.

One day Ahaziah fell off a balcony on the roof of his palace and was seriously injured. He sent messengers to ask his false god Baalzebub if he would get better. Elijah was angry that the king had not prayed to God instead.

'You will not get better. You will die,' was God's message to the king through Elijah.

What a tragic end to the life of a wicked man.

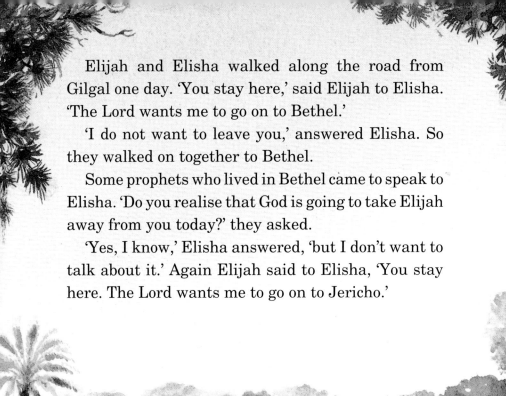

Elijah and Elisha walked along the road from Gilgal one day. 'You stay here,' said Elijah to Elisha. 'The Lord wants me to go on to Bethel.'

'I do not want to leave you,' answered Elisha. So they walked on together to Bethel.

Some prophets who lived in Bethel came to speak to Elisha. 'Do you realise that God is going to take Elijah away from you today?' they asked.

'Yes, I know,' Elisha answered, 'but I don't want to talk about it.' Again Elijah said to Elisha, 'You stay here. The Lord wants me to go on to Jericho.'

Again Elisha insisted on going with him. The prophets at Jericho had the same message for Elisha and he gave the same answer. Elijah had to move on to the River Jordan. Still Elisha insisted on going with him. Fifty prophets followed them.

Elijah and Elisha stopped on the river bank. Elijah took off his cloak, rolled it up and struck the water with it. The water divided and he and Elisha walked across the river bed to the other side.

'Tell me what you want me to do for you before I am taken away,' Elijah asked Elisha.

'Let me be given a double portion of your power,' answered Elisha. 'That will be difficult to grant,' Elijah replied. 'You will receive it only if you see me as I am taken up to heaven in the whirlwind.' They kept talking as they walked along. Suddenly a chariot of fire, pulled by horses of fire came between them. Elijah was taken up to heaven by a whirlwind.

Elisha was a witness to this wonderful happening. He tore his own cloak in two in his grief. He picked up Elijah's cloak and carried it back to the bank of the Jordan. He struck the water with the cloak twice, and it divided. Then Elisha walked over to the other side.

The fifty prophets realised that the power of God was now with Elisha.

Elijah stood up for what was right in very difficult circumstances. God came first in his life and His word was most important.

God's word is important for us too. It can guide us in difficult times, it can comfort us when we are sad. It encourages us to do God's will. In it we learn about Jesus Christ and how He died to save us from sin.